INSTRUCTOR'S GUIDE

EMERGENCY MANAGEMENT EXERCISES:
FROM RESPONSE TO RECOVERY

Everything you need to know to design a great excercise

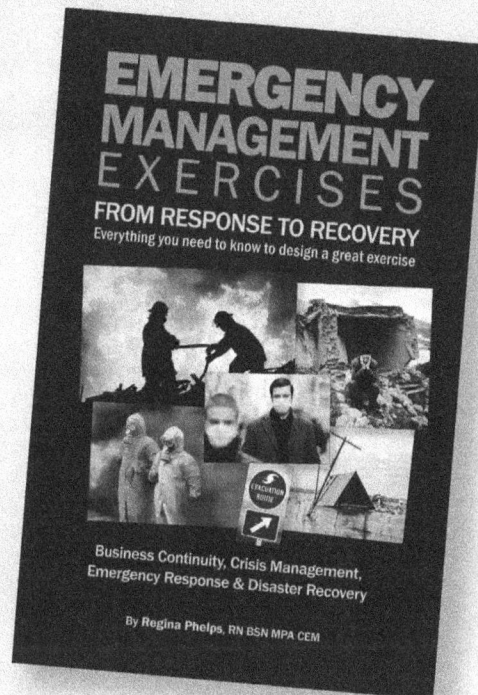

EMERGENCY MANAGEMENT EXERCISES
E X E R C I S E S
FROM RESPONSE TO RECOVERY
Everything you need to know to design a great exercise

Business Continuity, Crisis Management,
Emergency Response & Disaster Recovery

By Regina Phelps, RN BSN MPA CEM

By **Regina Phelps**, RN BSN MPA CEM
President and Founder Emergency Management & Safety Solutions Inc.

Chandi Media

www.ChandiMedia.com

260 Whitney Street
San Francisco, CA 94131

415-643-4300 (voice)

INSTRUCTOR'S GUIDE
EMERGENCY MANAGEMENT EXERCISES: FROM RESPONSE TO RECOVERY
Everything you need to know to design a great exercise

Published by:

Chandi Media
260 Whitney Street
San Francisco, CA 94131
415-643-4300 (voice)
www.ChandiMedia.com
Info@ChandiMedia.com

ISBN: 978-0-9831143-2-1
LCCN: 2012942114

CONTENTS

The mediocre teacher tells. The good teacher explains. The superior teacher demostrates. The great teacher inspires.

-William A Ward

CONTENTS

Continued from previous page

INTRODUCTION

Over my thirty-plus years of practice, I have designed thousands of exercises. I know clearly and understand the power of a well-designed exercise. Your decision to teach this class is an exciting one. You can make an enormous difference in your students' abilities to create a meaningful and impactful exercise. That ability, in turn, can have a major influence on their professional lives, their organizations' abilities to respond to a disaster, and, ultimately, the recovery of the communities in which they live.

And it all starts right here, in your classroom.

Enjoy the class and the students. You are making a real difference.

- Regina Phelps

"

It is the supreme art of the teacher to awaken joy in creative expression and knowledge.

"

- Albert Einstein

OVERVIEW

This Exercise Design course was intended to be taught over a 10- to 14-week period of time. The group activities can be lengthened or shortened to meet your specific class needs. The time can also be lengthened or shortened by adjusting the classroom assignments.

Adults learn by doing; this book and class are designed for just that. The reading assignments, combined with individual and group activities, will help students internalize the material. When they leave your classroom, they should be able to put their new knowledge into immediate practice.

The classroom activities were designed to be done by individuals; however, that may not work in your setting. Feel free to modify the activities to be done by a group if that better suits your needs. To assist you with group assignments, we have designed three mock companies that you can use for group exercises. You'll find them in the Appendix.

Nobody cares if you can't dance well. Just get up and dance. Great dancers are not great because of their technique; they are great because of their passion.

-Martha Graham

TEXTBOOK

"

The job of an educator is to teach students to see the vitality in themselves.

"

- Joseph Campbell

Required reading

▶ *Emergency Management Exercises: From Response To Recovery, Everything You Need To Know To Design a Great Exercise*
  ▷ Copyright © 2010 by Regina Phelps.
  ▷ First printing: October 2010.
  ▷ ISBN: 978-0-9831143-0-7.
  ▷ Published by Chandi Media, San Francisco, CA 94131, www.ChandiMedia.com. Also available from Amazon: http://tinyurl.com/7wvjb5r.

Optional reading

▶ FEMA Independent Study Program http://training.fema.gov/IS/
  ▷ The Emergency Management Institute (EMI) offers self-paced courses designed for people who have emergency management responsibilities and the general public. All are offered free of charge to those who qualify for enrollment.
    > An Introduction to Exercises: IS – 120.a.
    > Exercise Evaluation and Improvement IS – 130.
    > Exercise Design: IS – 139.

SUMMARY OF ASSIGNMENTS

Students will be required to develop all of the associated materials for an exercise they would likely conduct at their employer or as a volunteer project (for example, for a not-for-profit organization). The goal of this interactive process is for each student to learn the details and intricacies of how to design exercises for the real world. The exercise designed in this class should be of the quality that could be delivered at a real company – their place of work or a volunteer assignment. The exercise should also help the response team experiencing the exercise to meet their goals, build their team, and expand their knowledge. It should be "good to go" at the end of this course.

Individual work assignments

ASSIGNMENT	WEEK ASSIGNED	WEEK DUE
Develop an exercise design team.	Week 2	Week 3
Develop an exercise plan (Part 2).	Week 3	Week 4
Develop the exercise plan assumptions, artificialities, and narrative (Part 2).	Week 4	Week 5
Develop at least 10 exercise injects that support the exercise plan.	Week 5	Week 6
Revise all injects from the previous week based on this week's class and feedback. Add at least five new ones (total of at least 15 injects).	Week 6	Week 7
Develop five more injects (total of at least 20 injects).	Week 7	Week 8
Develop observer and participant evaluation forms, phone directory, executive briefing materials, and a document summary.	Week 8	Week 9
Based on exercise discussions and feedback, refine the exercise packet. Next week, hand in final exercise documents. These include: • Exercise plan. • Exercise injects. • Observer form. • Participant evaluation form. •Phone directory (if designing a functional exercise). • Document summary.	Week 9	Week 10
Write one essay question (1,500 words).	Week 10	Week 12
Continue writing one essay question (1,500 words) (due Week 12).	Week 11	Week 12
Develop an exercise project plan and a one-year exercise calendar to support exercise development.	Week 12	Week 13
Develop the outline for the after-action report following the exercise. Write an executive summary and develop one recommendation (one that you think will likely be made).	Week 13	Week 14

SUMMARY OF ASSIGNMENTS continued on next page

SUMMARY OF ASSIGNMENTS continued from the previous page

Individual project grading

The following are suggestions for grading this course. Grading should be evaluated based on completion of the individual assignments as described below:

Deliverable: Complete exercise materials

All required exercise material items are present:

Exercise plan:
- ☐ Exercise injects.
- ☐ Any additional A-V materials.
- ☐ Observer form.
- ☐ Executive briefing.
- ☐ Participant evaluation.
- ☐ Phone directory.

Exercise plan is complete:
- ☐ Type and scope.
- ☐ Goal.
- ☐ Objectives.
- ☐ Agenda.
- ☐ Instructions to the participants.
- ☐ Communication.
- ☐ Evaluation.
- ☐ Artificialities and assumptions.
- ☐ Narrative.

Narrative:
- ☐ Narrative is realistic.
- ☐ Narrative is appropriate in size and tone for the company or entity.
- ☐ Narrative contains all appropriate information for the response team to use.

Injects cover main themes:
- ☐ People.
- ☐ Facilities.
- ☐ Technology.

SUMMARY OF ASSIGNMENTS continued on next page

SUMMARY OF ASSIGNMENTS continued from the previous page

☐ Mission-critical activities at risk.

☐ Communication.

All materials presented must show command of the material, including understanding the utility of the exercise item and the student's approach to its design.

Deliverable: Essay question

The 1,500-word essay due Week 12 should be graded on:

☐ Command of the material.

☐ Strength of the argument for an exercise program

☐ Clarity of the student's understanding of an exercise program

☐ Demonstrated knowledge of the value of exercises

Deliverable: Class participation

Students are expected to participate in class discussions by responding to the week's discussion questions. Participation should be graded according to:

☐ Command of the week's material.

☐ Understanding of the discussion question.

☐ Appropriateness of response.

☐ Interaction with the instructor and other students (as appropriate).

> "
> *I am not
> a teacher, but
> an awakener.*
> "
>
> *- Robert Frost*

WEEK 1

Topics: Why do exercises? The six types of exercises

Why do exercises? What is the expected outcome? This week the class digs into the rationale behind exercise programs – what can be gained from well-designed exercises and why they should be held.

Objectives

By the end of this week's discussion, the student should be able to review:
▶ The benefits of an exercise program.
▶ The six different types of exercises.
▶ The different types of effective exercise schedules.

Required reading

▶ *Emergency Management Exercises: From Response To Recovery, Everything You Need To Know To Design a Great Exercise,* Chapters 1 and 2.

Discussion topics

Question # 1

Watch this video on rewards, motivation, and performance:
http://www.ted.com/talks/lang/eng/dan_pink_on_motivation.html

Some companies insist that emergency response exercises be considered as true tests, with pass/fail outcomes. Others maintain that all exercise learnings are good, and so no "grade" needs to be issued. After viewing the video, which do you support? How would you suggest a company should set up an exercise that would get people to perform well?

Question # 2

All companies want their response teams to be well-oiled machines, able to respond to any event with competence. One way to approach this is to keep the team as cohesive as possible, so they learn to work well with each other through practice. Another way is to rotate team members so that more people can learn their roles through following established processes. Discuss the pluses and minuses of each approach.

WEEK 2

Topics: Your secret weapon – The Exercise Design Team

Many emergency management professionals say they design their exercises by themselves. It doesn't matter how smart they are, how long they have been at the organization, or how many exercises they have done in the past, they can't know or think of everything. In the opinion of the book's author, the best exercises use a design team. What makes an exercise hit home and really sizzle is a narrative and highly specific injects[1] tailored to the inner workings of the company. The emergency management professionals can't do that alone; they need some help. The design team has two main jobs: to validate the narrative, and to develop the exercise injects. This topic covers who should be on the team and how to manage team members to get the desired results.

Objectives

By the end of this week's discussion, the student should be able to review:
- ▶ The benefits of an exercise design team.
- ▶ The composition of the exercise design team.
- ▶ A typical design team meeting format and agenda.

Required reading

- ▶ *Emergency Management Exercises: From Response To Recovery, Everything You Need To Know To Design a Great Exercise,* Chapters 3 and 7.

Discussion topics

Question # 1

You are in a small organization, and everyone who would be a great exercise design team member is participating in the exercise. You don't want to tell them the narrative, yet you need their expertise to design the narrative and injects. What options do you have? Could you use other staff? How could you use them without telling them the story?

Question # 2

You are developing a list of likely exercise design team members. Your manager says you should have senior managers on the team to lend credibility. What do you think of that? What would be the advantages? Would there be any negative aspects of having senior managers on the team?

---

1   Exercise injects are Information provided to players that requires action or stimulates discussion. They move the story past the initial baseline narrative and simulate reality.

WEEK 2 continued on next page

WEEK 2 continued from previous page

Reminders

Individual assignment
Due Week 3:
- ▶ Develop an exercise design team. Specify who will be on it and their titles.
- ▶ Develop the exercise design team meeting schedule and agendas.

WEEK 3

Topic: The exercise plan (Part 1)

The exercise plan is the backbone of the exercise event. It contains everything the participant needs to know to "play." A carefully crafted exercise plan is essential for a successful experience. It should answer, "Why are we doing this exercise?" over and over again. The exercise designer must keep asking that question in the development of this plan, in order to keep the exercise design and the team on track.

Objectives

By the end of this week's discussion, the student should be able to review the exercise:
- ▶ Type and scope.
- ▶ Goal.
- ▶ Agenda.
- ▶ Objectives.
- ▶ Communication.
- ▶ Evaluation tools.
- ▶ Instructions to the participants.

Required reading

- ▶ *Emergency Management Exercises: From Response To Recovery, Everything You Need To Know To Design a Great Exercise,* Chapter 4.

Discussion topics

Question # 1

You are organizing an exercise for your company (or your client, or an organization with which you work closely). You ask the basic question, "Why are we doing this exercise?" The team responds, "Because we've been told we have to." That's a valid reason for them, but it doesn't get the kind of answer needed to design the right narrative. How do you get them to a different answer than "we have to"?

Question # 2

When doing an exercise, some companies will allow the exercise participants to call a real company department in order to find out information. Some want all calls from the exercise participants to go to the simulation team. Which would you choose? Why?

WEEK 3 continued on next page

WEEK 3 continued from previous page

Reminders

Individual assignment
Due Week 4:

▶ Develop an exercise plan (Part One).

▷ See Appendix for Exercise Plan template and sample.

WEEK 4

Topics: The exercise plan (Part 2)

Once the basic exercise plan – the skeleton or core structure for the exercise – has been developed and "Why are you doing this?" is clear, then it is time to start designing the narrative. The narrative is the baseline story that gets the team started. It is like reading a draft screenplay or the opening chapter of a book. It tells the participants everything they need to know to get started.

The narrative is composed of three parts: assumptions, artificialities, and the narrative proper. Depending on the type of exercise and when the "exercise clock" begins, the exercise narrative can be short or quite long. The key thing to keep in mind is that if the players aren't told something, they won't know if something has happened. It is in this "gray zone" that participants will be inclined to make their own assumptions about how things have been handled. The more complete and realistic a story that can be painted for them, the less likely they will be to invent their own versions of the story and, potentially, derail the exercise.

Objectives

By the end of this week's discussion, the student should be able to review the exercise:

▶ Narrative.
▶ Assumptions.
▶ Artificialities.

Required reading

▶ *Emergency Management Exercises: From Response To Recovery, Everything You Need To Know To Design a Great Exercise,* Chapter 5.

Optional reading

▶ An Introduction to Exercises: IS – 120.a. This is a web-based course located on the FEMA website. http://training.fema.gov/EMIWeb/IS/is120a.asp
  ▷ Complete the Overview – Lesson 2.

Discussion topics

The narrative is a key element of the exercise, so a variety of issues could be explored in its design. Select one or two of the following questions you feel are most appropriate for the students in your class to answer.

WEEK 4 continued on next page

WEEK 4 continued from previous page

Question # 1

Does the exercise have to revolve around a "hard" incident, like a fire or explosion? Can the exercise narrative revolve around a "soft" incident, such as a security breach or an event that generates bad press for the company? Why or why not? How would they be similar? How would they differ? Discuss the pluses and minuses of choosing either narrative.

Question # 2

Some exercise narratives state that the event is happening "now" or "today"; others state that it is "next Tuesday" or some other date in the future, or even in the past. Discuss why one would be chosen versus the other. Discuss some of the pros and cons of artificially moving the date versus keeping it on the day of the event.

Question # 3

How do you decide if/when a narrative is too "small" or too "big"? For some companies, a flood may be a minor issue; for others, it could be catastrophic. A catastrophic event narrative will certainly motivate the participants – but it could easily overwhelm them, to the point of being useless. Discuss your thought process on determining "how much is too much." Will it vary by location, or can it be used across the company?

Question # 4

Has anything happened in your city/county recently that would provide a good narrative to use for an exercise? Describe it and discuss how you would modify it to fit your situation, or discuss why you think it wouldn't work for your situation even if it were modified.

Question # 5

What elements of a narrative do you believe to be the most important? Is it the time frame? The people involved? Discuss how you think you should approach crafting a narrative for your situation, and what key points you believe you should focus on.

Reminders

Individual assignment

Due Week 5:
  ▶ Develop the exercise plan assumptions, artificialities and narrative (Part 2).

WEEK 5

Topic: Developing the Exercise Injects

Once the exercise plan is developed and the narrative set, the focus of the design turns to the development of injects. This is where the exercise design team comes into play. The design team, composed of company subject-matter experts, helps ensure that exercise injects – information or problems coming in to the exercise participants – are highly specific, focused on particular business issues, and help meet exercise objectives.

As their name implies, exercise injects are "injected" into the exercise at different times to move the story line along, push the team to new learnings and experiences, and to focus on the exercise objectives. For example, if an exercise objective is about media communications and the preparation of press releases and talking points, several injects should be from members of the media (radio stations, newspaper reporters) asking for the company's official response to the incident.

Injects can cascade and build upon each other. For example, an earthquake can lead to a gas leak, which leads to an explosion, which leads to a collapsed building.

As the exercise designer, your challenge is to keep focused on the "Why are we doing this?" question so that the exercise objectives are met, the narrative and injects stay on target, and the goal or vision of the exercise is maintained.

Objectives

By the end of this week's discussion, the student should be able to:

▶ Detail the components of an effective exercise inject.

Required reading

▶ *Emergency Management Exercises: From Response To Recovery Everything You Need To Know To Design a Great Exercise*, Chapter 6.

Optional reading

▶ An Introduction to Exercises: IS – 120.a. This is a web-based course located on the FEMA website. http://training.fema.gov/EMIWeb/IS/is120a.asp
▷ Complete Lesson 3 – Lesson 5.

Discussion topics

Question # 1

Two members of your design team represent mission-critical departments that you are only somewhat familiar with. They are important subject-matter experts, but they are not

WEEK 5 continued on next page

WEEK 5 continued from previous page

participating fully in the design process and have given you only a few lackluster injects that don't really challenge the exercise team. Discuss ways you can draw more and better injects from them.

Question # 2

Your exercise is rapidly approaching, and you only have time for two design team meetings. How would you structure those two meetings to make the most of them? Of the five "buckets" of inject topics (people, facilities, technology, mission-critical activities at risk, communications), which do you think is most important to develop injects for? Which ones make for the best exercise? Why?

Reminders

Individual assignment

Due Week 6:

▶ Develop at least 10 exercise injects that support your exercise plan.

WEEK 6

Topic: Refining the Exercise Injects

Well-written injects are critical to making the exercise deliver the desired impact. The next two weeks will be spent reviewing and refining injects in class. This may seem like overkill or a waste of time, but each one needs to be reviewed carefully and in detail. Is the wording right? Does it answer the question, "Why are we doing this?" Is the routing (i.e., who should receive the inject) correct and thoughtful? Classes 6 and 7 can be run just like a design team. Students share their injects and the team discusses their strengths, weaknesses, and areas for improvement.

Objectives

By the end of this week's discussion, the student should be able to:

▶ Detail the components of an effective exercise inject.
▶ Describe the different ways to present injects into an exercise.
▶ Name the sources for exercise information.
▶ Identify the five topics that injects should address in an exercise.

Required reading

▶ No required reading this week.

Optional reading

▶ An Introduction to Exercises: IS – 120.a. This is a web-based course located on the FEMA website. http://training.fema.gov/EMIWeb/IS/is120a.asp
▷ Complete Lesson 6 – Lesson 7.

Discussion topics

Question # 1

What makes a good inject "good"? What are its attributes and hallmarks? List the findings and discuss.

Question # 2

What makes an inject "less than" (of lesser quality)? What makes it miss the mark? Peel back well written and less-than-well-written injects. Review and discuss the qualities that separate them. What can be done in design team meetings to get better injects from the team? Ask students to share their good ones and the ones that they plan to rework.

WEEK 6 continued on next page

WEEK 6 continued from previous page

Reminders

Individual assignment
Due Week 7:
▶ Revise all injects from last week, based on this week's class and feedback. Add at least five new ones, for a total of at least 15 injects.

WEEK 7

Topic: One more look at injects

This last session on injects is all about refinement. The goal is that by the end of this session, the student's injects are "water-tight" and ready to go – they could be used in the exercise without further modification.

Objectives

By the end of this week's discussion, the student should be able to:

▶ Detail the components of an effective exercise inject.
▶ Describe the different ways to present injects into an exercise.
▶ Name the sources for exercise information.
▶ Identify the five topics that injects should address in an exercise.

Required reading

▶ No required reading this week.

Optional reading

▶ Exercise Design: IS – 139. This Independent Study (IS) program can be downloaded from the FEMA website. http://training.fema.gov/emiweb/is/is139lst.asp
  ▷ Complete the Overview – Unit 4.

Discussion topics

Question # 1

Which are "good" injects to start off an exercise? Which ones should be saved for the end? Discuss the flow of an exercise and the way injects influence the exercise activity.

Question # 2

How many injects are sufficient in an exercise? What can be done if there aren't enough and the energy of the group lags? What can be done if there are too many?

Reminders

Individual assignment

Due Week 8:

▶ Develop at least five more injects, creating a final set of at least 20 injects.

WEEK 8

Topic: Keeping track of it all

Week 8 contains all of those "loose ends" that are important to complete the exercise design. These loosely connected topics include:

▶ A/V tools.
▶ Simulation team.
▶ Phone directory.
▶ Forms:
▶ Participant evaluations.
▶ Evaluators/Observers (E/O).
▶ Message center forms.
▶ Document summary.

Objectives

By the end of this week's discussion, the student should be able to:

▶ Identify appropriate audio-visual tools to inject information into the exercise.
▶ Identify the information necessary to select and train a simulation team, observers, and evaluators.
▶ Develop necessary documents to complete the exercise packet, including:
    ▷ Participant evaluation forms.
    ▷ Observer evaluation forms.
    ▷ Phone directory.
    ▷ Document summary form.

Required reading

▶ *Emergency Management Exercises: From Response To Recovery, Everything You Need To Know To Design a Great Exercise,* Chapters 8 and 9.

Optional reading

▶ Exercise Design: IS – 139. This Independent Study (IS) program can be downloaded from the FEMA website. http://training.fema.gov/emiweb/is/is139lst.asp
    ▷ Complete Unit 5 – Unit 8.

Optional activity

▶ Play2Train emergency response simulation.

Play2Train is a virtual reality community developed to teach emergency managers how to respond during a disaster. Watch the video at the bottom of this web page to learn

WEEK 8 continued on next page

WEEK 8 continued from previous page

more. http://play2train.us/wordpress/?cat=16

Discussion topics

Question # 1

Evaluators are an important part of the exercise assessment. How many should be at an exercise? What makes a good evaluator, and why? Which kinds of comments are helpful? Which comments are not? What if the evaluator primarily critiques individuals unfavorably? How is that handled with the evaluator? With the team?

Question # 2

Your exercise design team has developed eight "key" injects to the exercise; however, you only have one assigned evaluator/observer, who is not able to monitor all eight injects. Discuss possible ways you can still keep track of all injects.

Reminders

Individual assignment

Due Week 9:

▶ Develop observer and participant evaluation forms, phone directory (if developing a functional exercise), and a document summary.

WEEK 9

Topic: Exercise day

All the work is done, and the big day has finally arrived. This week covers how to manage the exercise experience and how to deal with all of the last-minute things that are likely to come up. This session includes:
- ▶ Managing exercise day.
- ▶ Managing the simulation team.
- ▶ Keeping your eye on everything – using observers to expand your vision.
- ▶ Debriefing the exercise – a critical part of the day.

Objectives

By the end of this week's discussion, the student should be able to:
- ▶ Set the tone for success with a strong exercise briefing.
- ▶ Identify ways to keep the simulation team on track.
- ▶ Develop tools for successful observations during the exercise.
- ▶ Learn ways to manage an exercise that starts to go "sideways," and learn how to correct it on the fly.
- ▶ Learn how to conduct an exercise debriefing to get the information that you need for team and plan improvement.

Required reading

- ▶ *Emergency Management Exercises: From Response To Recovery, Everything You Need To Know To Design a Great Exercise*, Chapters 10 and 11.

Optional reading

- ▶ Exercise Design: IS – 139. This IS program can be downloaded from the FEMA website. http://training.fema.gov/emiweb/is/is139lst.asp
  - ▷ Complete Unit 9 – Appendix C.

Discussion topics

Question # 1

Your manager has asked that you give out the exercise plan at least 24 hours in advance of the exercise so participants can be more prepared. What would be the pros of giving out the plan in advance? What are the disadvantages? Develop a response that outlines why this might be a good idea, and why it might be a bad idea. Discuss all of the options, select one, and then build your case to present to your manager.

WEEK 9 continued on next page

WEEK 9 continued from previous page

Question # 2

During the exercise, the simulation team continues to be stonewalled by exercise participants. They reply to injects with responses like, "We've already fixed that," "The situation wasn't that bad," or "We called the vendor and got what we needed." You know none of those responses reflect reality. How do you get the exercise back on track? How to you keep the players on task and solving the problems rather than "blowing off" the injects? Discuss options for making the exercise work, getting the participants to really work on solving the issues, and keeping the atmosphere appropriate for learning.

Reminders

Individual assignment

Due Week 10:

▶ Based on exercise discussions and feedback, refine the exercise packet. Next week, hand in the final exercise documents, which include:

▷ Exercise plan.

▷ Exercise injects (at least 20).

▷ Observer form.

▷ Participant evaluation form.

▷ Phone directory (if designing a functional exercise).

▷ Document summary.

WEEK 10

Topics: Class presentations

The exercise is complete, and it's show time – now what? Each student gets an opportunity to present his or her exercise to the class. This gives the student:

▶ An opportunity to practice delivering the exercise plan to an audience.
▶ Feedback on the design.
▶ Feedback on the injects.

It also gives all of the students in the class new ideas about design, narratives, and injects.

Format: Class presentations

Have each student present the following material (no more than 7 – 10 minutes):

▶ Exercise type.
▶ Exercise goal.
▶ Exercise scope.
▶ Exercise objectives.
▶ Exercise narrative.
▶ Deliver three injects.

Objectives

By the end of this week's discussion, the student should be able to:

▶ Identify a well-designed exercise plan and injects.
▶ Provide feedback to fellow students.
▶ Learn new ideas for narratives and injects.

Required reading

▶ No required reading this week.

Optional reading

▶ Exercise Evaluation and Improvement IS – 130. This interactive, web-based program is located on the FEMA website. http://training.fema.gov/EMIWeb/IS/IS130.a
  ▷ Complete Lesson 1 – Lesson 3.

Discussion topics

There are no formal questions this week. Lead short discussions after each presentation on the strengths of the exercise plan and injects, and discuss areas for improvement.

WEEK 10 continued on next page

WEEK 10 continued from previous page

Reminders

Individual assignment

Due Week 12 (no assignment due on Week 11):

▶ Write an essay (1,500 words) on "The Value of a Comprehensive Exercise Program." The paper should build a case for an exercise program in an organization, describing the training and cost/benefit rationale for having a regular exercise program as part of a comprehensive emergency management program. Imagine that this is building a case with management, and the paper is the foundation for the discussion.

WEEK 11

Topics: Class presentations, continued
▶ Class presentations continue.

Format: Class presentations
Have each student present the following material (no more than 7 – 10 minutes):
▶ Exercise type.
▶ Exercise goal.
▶ Exercise scope.
▶ Exercise objectives.
▶ Exercise narrative.
▶ Deliver three injects.

Objectives
By the end of this week's discussion, the student should be able to:
▶ Identify a well-designed exercise plan and injects.
▶ Provide feedback to fellow students.
▶ Learn new ideas for narratives and injects.

Required reading
▶ No required reading this week.

Optional reading
▶ Exercise Evaluation and Improvement IS – 130. This interactive, web-based program is located on the FEMA website. http://training.fema.gov/EMIWeb/IS/IS130.a
  ▷ Complete Lesson 4 – Lesson 6.

Discussion topics
There are no formal questions this week. Lead short discussions after each presentation on the strengths of the exercise plan and injects, and discuss areas for improvement.

Reminders

Individual Assignment
Due Week 12:
▶ Write an essay (1,500 words) on "The Value of a Comprehensive Exercise Pro-

WEEK 11 continued on next page

WEEK 11 continued from previous page

gram." The paper should build a case for an exercise program in an organization, describing the training and cost/benefit rationale for having a regular exercise program as part of a comprehensive emergency management program. Imagine that this is building a case with management, and the paper is the foundation for the discussion.

WEEK 12

Topics: Exercise project plans and exercise calendars

This week digs into the details of making it all happen, looking at the three most common exercises (Orientation, Tabletop, and Functional) and formulating the project plans. The goal is to deeply understand how to bring the exercise into reality by clear structure and easy planning. Those concepts will also be used when discussing the idea of annual exercise calendars. The planning calendar is helpful to ensure that the exercise program is not only regular and robust, but also works well for all aspects of emergency management and business continuity management.

Objectives

By the end of this week's discussion, the student should be able to:
▶ Identify project plans to support three basic exercise styles (Orientation, Tabletop, and Functional).
▶ Identify the keys to project planning success.
▶ Develop strategies to ensure exercise success planning.
▶ Review the benefits of exercise program calendars.

Required reading

▶ *Emergency Management Exercises: From Response To Recovery, Everything You Need To Know To Design a Great Exercise*, Chapters 12, 13, 14, and 16.

Optional reading

▶ Exercise Evaluation and Improvement IS – 130. This interactive, web-based program is located on the FEMA website. http://training.fema.gov/EMIWeb/IS/IS130.a
  ▷ Complete Lesson 7 – Lesson 8.

Discussion topics

Question # 1

What are the contributing factors that lead to selecting a certain style of exercise? Which exercise should you begin with? When is a team ready to progress to a more sophisticated form? How often should you exercise the team to build "muscle memory"?

Question # 2

What are the benefits of a planned exercise program? How will this help build support

WEEK 12 continued on next page

for your overall program? Who are the likely sponsors of such a planning activity? Discuss ways to build support for your program in your company.

Reminders

Individual assignment

Due Week 13:

▶ Design and develop an exercise project plan for the exercise that you planned during this course (this includes work during Weeks 3 – 8).

▶ Develop a sample one-year exercise calendar.

WEEK 13

Topics: The after-action report, follow-up, and process improvements

The exercise is complete, and it was a rousing success – now what? How do the exercise results get turned into concrete plan changes, making the necessary modifications to processes that were identified in the exercise? Now the real work begins. This session talks about the development of the after action-report and the importance of timely exercise follow-up. This week's topics include:

▶ Writing an effective after-action report.
▶ Developing a plan of action to follow-up on identified issues.
▶ Getting the report and process improvements in front of the right people.

Objectives

By the end of this week's discussion, the student should be able to:

▶ Identify the components of a well-written after-action report.
▶ Develop follow-up tracking tools to chart progress towards program improvement.
▶ Develop ways to get the after action-report in front of the decision-makers.

Required reading

▶ *Emergency Management Exercises: From Response To Recovery, Everything You Need To Know To Design a Great Exercise*, Chapter 15.

Discussion topics

Question # 1

During the exercise, you discover that many of the issues raised are tied to a particular senior person in the company. This was brought out in the exercise injects, the debrief, and the written participant evaluations. Some of the feedback is quite blunt, but other comments are more indirect. How do you handle this in the after-action report? Do you say anything about it in the facilitator observations or executive summary? Or is that akin to a "CLM" (career-limiting move)? How do you direct attention to the problem while not losing your job in the process?

Question # 2

You have been selected to present your exercise findings to the Corporate Risk Committee. This body of senior company executives has given you 15 minutes to present your findings. Your boss says you can have no more than 4 slides. How will you use this time?

WEEK 13 continued on next page

WEEK 13 continued from previous page

How can you use this to advance the emergency management/business continuity program in the company? Are there things you shouldn't talk about? Discuss what you want to get out of this session, and how you plan to go about it.

Reminders

Individual assignment

Due Week 14:

▶ Develop an outline for the after-action report for the in-class exercise. Write the executive summary, and develop one recommendation that you think will likely be made as a result of the exercise.

WEEK 14

Topics: Class wrap-up

The class is over – now what? This is your great opportunity to go back and revisit the highlights of the class and to inspire your class into action.

Objectives

By the end of this week's discussion, the student should be able to:

▶ Review the highlights of a successful exercise program and plan.

▶ Explore stumbling blocks and opportunities for growth while moving forward in implementing an exercise program.

▶ Explore ways to make it fresh and exciting so that the exercise players want to keep coming back.

▶ Conduct a debriefing of the class: What worked well? What needs improvement?

Discussion topics

Question # 1

You have done three exercises with your team, an Orientation, an Advanced Tabletop, and a Functional exercise. Your manager asks what else you can do to make it interesting and inspiring for the exercise players. What is your reply?

Question # 2

Sometimes the response to shaking up an exercise program is to get "really creative." What are the pluses and minuses to a "really creative" approach? Go back and revisit the "big question" as a way of discussing this topic. (The discussion regarding "Big Question" is located in Chapter Four of the required textbook.)

Question # 3

Take at least 15 minutes of class to conduct your own debrief of the experience, and ask the two questions that we use in exercises: What worked well? What needs improvement?

EPILOGUE

Congratulations! You have completed the course and have prepared and sent your students off into the world to make a difference. Take time now to make notes on how you might lead the class differently (What worked? What needs improvement?) so you will be ready to go next time. Kudos!

APPENDIX

The appendix includes materials that may be helpful in your classroom instruction. This section includes:

▶ Exercise plan template.

▶ Exercise plan sample.

▶ Exercise inject template.

▶ Mock company information sheets.

APPENDIX
Exercise plan template

Here is an exercise plan template for your students to fill in, to build their individual assignment exercise.

1. Exercise type and scope
- ▶ Bullet 1.
- ▶ Bullet 2.
- ▶ Bullet 3.

2. Exercise goal
Exercise goal.

3. Exercise agenda

TIME	ACTIVITY	LEADER
Start – End	Activity name	Leader name
Start – End	Activity name	Leader name
Start – End	Activity name	Leader name
Start – End	Activity name	Leader name
Start – End	Activity name	Leader name

4. Exercise objectives
- a. Objective 1.
- b. Objective 2.
- c. Objective 3.
- d. Objective 4.
- e. Objective 5.

5. Instructions to participants
- ▶ Instruction 1.
- ▶ Instruction 2.
- ▶ Instruction 3.
- ▶ Instruction 4.

EXERCISE PLAN TEMPLATE continued on next page

EXERCISE PLAN TEMPLATE continued from previous page

▶ Instruction 5.

6. Communications
▶ Communication instruction 1.
▶ Communication instruction 2.
▶ Communication instruction 3.
▶ Communication instruction 4.
▶ Communication instruction 5.

7. Evaluation
Evaluation information.

8. Exercise assumptions
▶ Assumption 1.
▶ Assumption 2.
▶ Assumption 3.
▶ Assumption 4.
▶ Assumption 5.

9. Exercise artificialities
▶ Artificiality 1.
▶ Artificiality 2.
▶ Artificiality 3.
▶ Artificiality 4.
▶ Artificiality 5.

10. Narrative
Exercise narrative, providing information to exercise participants (covered in Week 4).

APPENDIX
Exercise plan sample

Here is a sample of an exercise plan:

1. Exercise type and scope
▶ Functional exercise, using pre-scripted messages, a simulation team, and periodic media inputs.
▶ Activation of Finance Co.'s full Corporate Incident Response Team (CIRT). All other groups are simulated.
▶ One Executive Management briefing.

2. Exercise goal
The goal of this exercise is to experience a local San Francisco event impacting Finance Co.'s mission-critical Financial Management department, and assess the ability of the CIRT to manage the event.

3. Exercise agenda

TIME	ACTIVITY	LEADER
8:30 AM	Continental breakfast	
9:00 AM – 9:10 AM	Welcome and introductions	J. Smith, sponsor
9:10 AM – 12:00 PM	Exercise	R. Phelps, facilitator
12:00 PM – 12:15 PM	Executive briefing	S. Jones, Incident Commander
12:15 PM – 1:20 PM	Conclusion: ▶ Exercise debriefing ▶ Complete written evaluations	R. Phelps
1:20 PM – 1:30 PM	Next steps	J. Smith

4. Exercise objectives
a. Assess the effectiveness of the Incident Response Plan in dealing with this type of event. Note areas for improvement and modification.
b. Assess overall CIRT decisions and the Planning and Intelligence Team's ability to continue to provide mission-critical Financial Management operations in San Francisco when equipment and staff are not available to work from that location. Note areas for improvement and modification.
c. Assess the ability of the CIRT to develop the Finance Co. message, and produce the following communication materials: employee Hotline updates, employee communications via email and web, press releases, and customer notifications.
d. Assess effectiveness of the call notification system to reach all CIRT members. Assess CIRT members' ability to respond back in a timely manner (within 30 min-

EXERCISE PLAN SAMPLE continued on next page

EXERCISE PLAN SAMPLE continued from previous page

utes from the time of the call-out).

e. Assess the CIRT plan and the (EOC) facility for completeness.

5. Instructions to participants

▶ Exercises have the greatest value if they are treated as real. Stay in role the entire time.

▶ Don't just think about responding to what is coming at you – remember to keep one eye into the future and play the game of "what-if."

▶ As the exercise progresses, details may not be as complete as you would like. The value is in the process, the dialogue, and the experience. The design team has worked to make the situations as realistic as possible.

▶ You may use only what is in place as of today; if new equipment is being added next month, it can't be used.

▶ Exercises are for learning; expect mistakes. The goal is to develop the team and learn from the experience.

▶ In order to make this exercise work and to facilitate the learning process, a certain amount of "exercise magic" has been used. We ask you not to debate that something has happened, could have happened, or is available – it just is!

▶ Questions regarding the exercise should be directed to the exercise facilitator.

6. Communications

▶ A simulation team will act as the "outside world" for this exercise. All problems must be solved by calling the simulation team, acting as proxies for the outside world. This includes any call that you would make to find out information, order equipment, etc. You will also receive calls throughout the exercise from numerous entities.

▷ Use the phone directory to call the simulation team.

▶ All information in the narrative and that provided by the facilitators and simulation team is to be considered valid. However, just as in a real disaster, messages can be jumbled, and rumors can start on incorrect information or assumptions. Multiple versions of the same problem may occur.

7. Evaluation

The exercise will be evaluated by use of participants' written evaluations, the debrief session, and evaluators' observations based on the objectives.

EXERCISE PLAN SAMPLE continued on next page

EXERCISE PLAN SAMPLE continued from previous page

8. General exercise assumptions

▶ All information in the narrative is to be considered valid.

▶ All information provided by the facilitators is to be considered valid.

▶ Don't assume anything else. All information can be verified by asking the facilitator.

9. Scenario-specific artificialities

▶ The event occurred this morning at <<time>>.

▶ It is now <<time>>.

▶ The weather is <<describe>>.

10. Narrative

Use sample provided in Week 4.

Exercise inject template

This form is best elongated and developed in the landscape (horizontal) format.

CALL #	CALL TIME	SIM TEAM CALLER	CALL ROUTED TO:	WHOM SIM TEAM IS PORTRAYING	INJECT CONTENT
1	00:01	Mary S	P & I	Mayor Jones	[Text of inject]
2	00:05	Joe W	Logs	Bill Executive	[Text of inject]
3	00:10	Bert R	OPS	Sue Reporter	[Text of inject]

MOCK COMPANIES

The following company profiles may be used if you decide to do group exercise assignments.

▶ Assign a team of between 5 and 10 students to a group, and assign them to be one of the three mock companies.

▶ Have the students, as a group, design the exercise assignments as delineated in the weekly topics, using the mock company as the organization that will be going through the exercise.

MOCK COMPANIES
National Manufacturing, Inc.

Introduction and company history

National Manufacturing, Inc., (NASDAQ: NMI) is the U.S. leader in widget manufacturing. It has plants in 12 states, offering widgets ranging in size from 1 inch to 17 feet. It also offers consulting services for customers desiring assistance in installing and maintaining their new widgets.

From its beginnings in the Long Island, New York, garage of its charismatic founder, George Antrobus, in 1972, NMI grew to become the most familiar name in widget-making. George eventually abandoned New York in 1978 and moved the company to Ohio, where he quickly expanded to Kentucky, West Virginia, and Illinois by 1995. In the past five to seven years, rather than open more factories of its own, National Manufacturing has opted to buy out its competitors. Its "growth-by-purchase" has not always gone smoothly, with some plants' inventory systems still not talking to others; very often, the plants' links and data uploads to the corporate IT system don't work as expected.

People

▶ The company is headquartered in Cleveland, Ohio.
  ▷ Through their expansion, they have factories in the following states: Ohio, Michigan, Florida, Missouri, Georgia, North Carolina, Illinois, Pennsylvania, Indiana, Tennessee, Kentucky, and West Virginia.
▶ The company employs 12,500 direct employees.
  ▷ Approximately 35% are full-time employees, with the remainder working part-time.
  ▷ Part-time employees work primarily in the factories; full-time employees are primarily in the corporate office.
  ▷ In addition to the direct employees, there is a small contractor cohort, approximately 275, with many based at the Cleveland headquarters, particularly in the Technology Division.
  ▷ The factories are unionized. The current contract is due for renewal in three months.
▶ In an attempt to be on the cutting edge of widgets, NMI recently opened an additional factory in Europe.
  ▷ Their Dublin, Ireland, factory is a new, state-of-the-art, highly robotic facility.
▶ Organizational structure:
  ▷ The Risk Management Division reports up to the Operations Group, and houses the Business Continuity department and the Financial Risk department.
  ▷ The Environmental Health & Safety department reports to Human Resourc-

NATIONAL MANUFACTURING, INC. continued on next page

NATIONAL MANUFACTURING, INC. continued from previous page

es, which reports up to the Admin Group.

▷ The disaster recovery function is integrated into the Technology Division, with all Technology employees cross-trained to perform various recovery activities. It is not an optimal set-up, and the structure has not worked well during emergencies in the past; luckily, those emergencies were relatively minor.

Facilities

▶ The Cleveland headquarters complex:

▷ Three small buildings: 101 Main Street, 111 Main Street, and 121 Main Street. Most executives occupy the top three floors of 121 Main. The data center is also located in 121 Main.

▷ All were built at the same time in 1980, and are separated by one city block.

▷ 101 Main is 2 stories tall, 111 Main is 2 stories tall, and 121 Main is 3 stories tall.

▷ National Manufacturing owns the buildings and occupies all floors, with the exception of the ground floor of 101 Main.

> That floor is rented out to a restaurant, America's Bounty Buffet, and a DrugRite drugstore.

▷ There are small cafeterias on the 1st floor of 101 Main and 111 Main; the primary company cafeteria is on the 3rd floor of 121 Main.

> All cafeterias are outsourced to GrazeWell, a local food vendor. The smaller cafeterias have no cooking facilities, and offer only cold sandwiches and salads, while the primary cafeteria offers a pizza station, grill station, and display cooking station, in addition to cold sandwiches and salads.

▶ Cleveland's Main Street runs parallel to a major artery through the city.

▷ To the east, the NMI buildings overlook both the freeway and a small airport.

▷ To the west, they overlook a cruise dock, where pleasure ships leave for short dinner cruises, as well as multiple-day long Cuyahoga river cruises.

▶ There is a generator for each building; however, they have not been tested in over two years.

▷ The data center in 121 Main has two UPS systems, as well as its own generator.

▷ The data center generator has not been tested in two years; all power outages that the company has suffered have been short enough that the UPS have been able to handle them.

▶ There are 15 other locations in 13 states.

NATIONAL MANUFACTURING, INC. continued on next page

NATIONAL MANUFACTURING, INC. continued from previous page

▷ Fourteen are factories; one is a call center devoted to the consulting services side of the company.

▷ The factories are owned by NMI; the call center is a 10,000-square-foot rented space in Jacksonville, Florida, which shares its building with three other companies and a small Greenpeace office.

Emergency response program

▶ National has a fairly robust Emergency Response Program in place for their corporate facilities in Cleveland.

▷ They have enthusiastic floor wardens.

▷ They are required by law to hold one full-building fire drill a year.

> Above and beyond the annual drill, EHS and the floor wardens hold smaller drills once a month, rotating through the various floors.

▶ NMI has not been as successful rolling out a similar robust ERP in its outlying and acquired properties.

▷ Some acquired factories came with a reasonably strong ERP; those have been maintained.

▷ Most acquisitions had emergency programs ranging from poor to mediocre, and the company has not had much success bringing these up to the same level as the Main Street complex.

Mission-critical activities

▶ As with any widget-making company that wants to stay ahead of the pack, the primary business activity of National Manufacturing, Inc., is making the finest quality widgets at the lowest possible cost.

▷ This includes automating as many processes as possible, although this has been problematic for some of the smaller widgets.

▷ Due to the widespread use of widgets in everything from cellphones to houses, there can be disastrous results if a widget is manufactured improperly.

> This can include anything from faulty raw materials to improper weld points to an NMI consultant providing incorrect information to a client.

▷ In addition, the factory employs tight "just-in-time" build-and-ship methodologies. While this results in lower costs, it also means that all vendors and suppliers and the factory itself must "hum" in sync all the time.

> If there are manufacturing delays, late shipment penalties can run into the thousands of dollars for every day that a delivery is behind schedule.

NATIONAL MANUFACTURING, INC. continued on next page

NATIONAL MANUFACTURING, INC. continued from previous page

Business continuity strategy

▶ The company has a contract with WeRent4U to provide a hotsite for National's technology recovery.
  ▷ The contract does not provide for a designated work area recovery space.
    > There is a provision for mobile work area trailers to be brought in.
    > The closest area large enough to accommodate the trailers is approximately one-half mile away from the Main Street building complex.
▶ The BCP program itself is still in its infancy, and was started by the Finance Manager three years ago.
  ▷ A rudimentary BIA was done then and has not been updated since.
  ▷ Bare-bones Business Continuity Plans were also created at that time, but have never been tested.
  ▷ All documentation was done in-house on Word documents and Excel spreadsheets. Formats vary from department to department.
  ▷ Other than experiencing a few peaceful union protests at the factories, there have been no significant disasters requiring the company to declare BCP activation since the company was formed.
▶ Factories are designed for specific sizes of widgets, and each factory makes one size. All factories can be refitted to manufacture the widget of another factory; however, no factory can manufacture more than one size of widget at a time.

Technology

▶ National's data center is housed in the 121 Main Street building.
  ▷ It occupies three-quarters of the floor, sharing the floor with the cafeteria.
  ▷ It contains more than 300 servers running 125 separate applications to serve the factories and various corporate processes.
  ▷ The Technology Division has outsourced their network services to eNetwerk.
    > Although support is outsourced, the network equipment still resides in this data center.
    > There is a project underway to move all networking equipment to an e-Netwerk facility in Detroit; this is due to be completed next month.
▶ The company runs an intranet and an extranet; they own the NationalManufactureInc.com domain.
  ▷ In order to protect their brand, they also own WeMakeWidgets.com, NMI.com, NatMan.com, and NatManInc.com. They also purchased the .net and .biz versions of these names.

NATIONAL MANUFACTURING, INC. continued on next page

NATIONAL MANUFACTURING, INC. continued from previous page

Disaster recovery strategy

▶ Approximately two months after the scheduled network move (see above), the entire data center is also scheduled to move into a new facility in Pittsburgh, Pennsylvania.

  ▷ With the network moving and the data center moving, no one seems to have noticed that the disaster recovery contract with WeRent4U is due to expire in three weeks.

▶ The WeRent4U contract provides hotsite services.

  ▷ The nearest hotsite location is in Toledo, Ohio.

  ▷ The contract does not provide for a designated work area recovery space.

  > There is a provision for mobile work area trailers to be brought in.

  > The closest area large enough to accommodate the trailers is approximately one-half mile away from the Main Street building complex.

▶ The DR strategy varies by system or application tier.

  ▷ Tier One application data is replicated in near-real-time to WeRent4U, with once daily tape back-ups sent to MoonGuard.

  > Only two applications are designated as Tier One (inventory reconciliation and customer contact).

  ▷ All other applications have tape back-ups taken either daily or weekly and sent to MoonGuard.

  > Although MoonGuard has facilities across the state, for ease of access, NMI has chosen to store its tapes at the MoonGuard facility two blocks south of the data center on Main Street.

  ▷ Recovery from tape has been tested for isolated applications, never more than one application at a time.

Communications

▶ Thanks to a plant manager who was found to be manufacturing unauthorized widgets on the side and flooding the black market with them, seriously undercutting the company's margin, the MarComm Division (Marketing and Communications) has recently contracted with two new communications and public relations specialists in addition to the existing two overworked specialists.

  ▷ The Division believes the need for these two additional specialists will be temporary.

NATIONAL MANUFACTURING, INC. continued on next page

NATIONAL MANUFACTURING, INC. continued from previous page

Crisis communications plan

▶ National Manufacturing has an informal crisis communications plan in place.

  ▷ There are very rough guidelines on what not to say and how not to say it.

  ▷ Overall, the Communications Department believes they can react quickly to any event that arises.

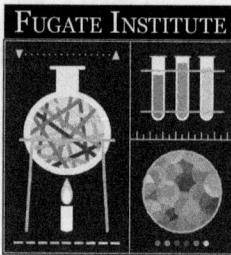

MOCK COMPANIES
Fugate Institute

Introduction and school history

Fugate Institute is a university with its primary campus located at 100 Washington Avenue, Indianapolis, Indiana. The school is noted for its research facilities, especially its work in genetics and infectious diseases. Its law school has recently become a center for social media legal matters.

Starting as a small academy for women in 1934 (The Barbara and Irene Charters Academy for Women) the school has grown through mergers with other local educational institutions. It currently includes the Todd College of Law (1948), the Phelps School of Public Health (1953), and the MacDonald School of Biological Sciences (1970). It was named Fugate thanks to its wealthy benefactor, J. Howard Williams, who named it after his wife's maiden name. Williams' son continues to take an active role in overseeing all research projects, much to the chagrin of the school's administration.

People

▶ The campus is headquartered in Indianapolis, Indiana. The Phelps School and the MacDonald School are located within the same 1,000 acres near the site of the former army base at Fort Benjamin Harrison. The Todd College of Law is located across the White River in the Fairfax neighborhood, not far from the Indianapolis Motor Speedway.

▶ The school population of approximately 16,000 is broken down as follows:
  ▷ Last year's student population was 6,000. Approximately 5,000 were full-time undergraduates; the remainder were graduate students. With few exceptions, most students live on campus.
  ▷ There are 10,000 direct employees working across the schools, in administrative functions, teaching faculty, and research operations support.

▶ Organizational structure:
  ▷ The Risk Management Division reports up to the Operations Group, and houses the Business Continuity Department and the Financial Risk Department.
  ▷ The Environmental Health & Safety Department reports to Human Resources, which reports up to the Admin Group.
  ▷ The disaster recovery function is integrated into the Technology Division, with all Technology employees cross-trained to perform various recovery activities. It is not an optimal set-up, and the structure has not worked well during emergencies in the past; luckily, those emergencies were relatively minor.

FUGATE INSTITUTE continued on next page

FUGATE INSTITUTE continued from previous page

Facilities

▶ The main Indianapolis campus address is 100 Washington Avenue, and is located on the banks of the White River, not far from the Indiana state government complex.

▷ There are 47 buildings over 1,000 acres:

> Fifteen dormitories. Most are six or seven stories tall, a few are three stories, and one is 10 stories.

> Seven administrative buildings, including libraries, student centers, and a bookstore. With the exception of three student centers scattered over the acreage, the four administration buildings are located on Washington Avenue (100, 105, 110, and 115 Washington Avenue).

> One brand-new building (Darwin Genetic Research Building), located in the middle of campus, is devoted to genetic research and contains eight state-of-the-art labs, including one used to study the relationship between nuclear fallout and human mutations.

> The remaining 25 buildings are combined teaching/research facilities.

> In addition to the eight new labs in Darwin, there are 32 other labs scattered throughout the educational buildings.

▷ Buildings range in age from the original Charters Academy buildings, built in 1934, to the Darwin Building, completed early this year.

▷ The older buildings are four or five stories; newer buildings are usually between five and 10 stories.

▷ Six parking structures are scattered around the campus. One is subterranean, the rest are multi-story.

▷ The Institute owns all buildings and occupies all floors, with the exception of the ground floor of the MacDonald Student Union.

> That floor is rented out to a restaurant, America's Bounty Buffet, a Drug-Rite drugstore, and a Java Junkie coffee shop.

▷ There are small cafeterias in each of the student centers, and a larger cafeteria in the 100 Washington Avenue building.

> All cafeterias are outsourced to GrazeWell, a local food vendor.

> The smaller cafeterias have no cooking facilities, and offer only cold sandwiches and salads, while the larger cafeteria offers a pizza station, grill station, and display cooking station, in addition to cold sandwiches and salads.

▷ Indianapolis' Washington Avenue runs parallel to an interstate that cuts the

FUGATE INSTITUTE continued on next page

FUGATE INSTITUTE continued from previous page

city into north and south.

> - To the east, two of the Institute's main administration buildings (100 and 105 Washington) overlook the state Capitol and Governor's mansion.
> - To the west, the 110 and 115 buildings overlook the White River and two cruise docks, where pleasure ships leave for short dinner cruises.

▷ There are generators for the library building, the Darwin Building, and one of the dorms; however, none of these have been tested in more than two years.

> - The data center in 100 Washington has two UPS systems as well as its own generator.
> - The data center generator has not been tested in two years, either; all power outages that the Institute has suffered have been short enough that the UPS have been able to handle them.

▶ The Todd College of Law is located across the White River in the Fairfax neighborhood, not far from the Indianapolis Motor Speedway.

▷ There are 4 buildings within a two-block area. The main address is 500 Brickyard Road.

> - All 4 buildings are multi-use, containing school administration, student union, and student housing functions.
> - The bookstore and library are in 500 Brickyard. Other buildings are 550 Brickyard, and 210 and 225 Speedway Drive.

▷ Three buildings are from the 1948-1950 era; one brand-new building (Fugate Law, at 225 Speedway Drive) was completed last year. Professors teaching in the Fugate Building specialize in social media legal defenses.

> - Two of the three older buildings do not have generators. The generator in the third building has not been tested in a year-and-a-half.
> - The new Fugate Building houses a small data center, and has a generator along with a UPS system for the data center. The generator has not been tested since the building was built last year.

Emergency response program

▶ The Fugate Institute staff has a fairly robust Emergency Response Program in place for their main administrative offices on Washington Avenue.

> - They have enthusiastic floor wardens.
> - They are required by law to hold one full-building fire drill a year.
> - Above and beyond the annual drill, EHS and the floor wardens hold smaller drills once a month, rotating through the various floors.

FUGATE INSTITUTE continued on next page

FUGATE INSTITUTE continued from previous page

▶ Fugate has not been as successful rolling out a similar robust ERP in its other buildings throughout both campus locations.
  ▷ The School of Law has put a reasonably strong ERP in place, but it does not get tested very often.
  ▷ The dorms rely on Resident Advisors (RAs) to coordinate and test building plans. Because it is a low priority to the RAs, few tests have been done.
  ▷ The programs that have been put in place in other buildings range from poor to mediocre, primarily due to the mixed-use nature of the buildings.

Mission-critical activities
▶ Although you may think that an educational institution's primary business activity is educating its students, in fact (as with any school with significant research facilities), the primary business activity of the Fugate Institute is maintaining research and research funding.
  ▷ One researcher works exclusively with primates, while three others focus on smaller creatures like fruit flies and worms. The remainder of the genetic research done in the labs is performed on mice and rabbits.
  ▷ The nuclear lab in the Darwin Building is relatively new, with only a few research projects underway; most are still in the preparatory stages of being funded. The professor and graduate students working here plan to do their testing on miniature pigs.

Business continuity strategy
▶ The company has a contract with WeRent4U to provide a hotsite for Fugate's technology recovery.
  ▷ The contract does not provide for a designated work area recovery space.
    > There is a provision for mobile work area trailers to be brought in.
    > The closest area large enough to accommodate the trailers is approximately one-half mile away (and across the river) from the Washington Avenue building complex.
▶ The BCP program itself is still in its infancy, and was started by the tenured genetics professor three years ago.
  ▷ A rudimentary BIA was done then and has not been updated since.
  ▷ Bare-bones Business Continuity Plans for each school were also created at that time but have never been tested.
  ▷ All documentation was done in-house on Word documents and Excel spread-

FUGATE INSTITUTE continued on next page

FUGATE INSTITUTE continued from previous page

sheets. Formats vary from school to school and from department to department.

▷ Other than experiencing an average of eight protests a year, usually from animal rights' activists, there have been no significant disasters requiring the company to declare BCP activation since the Institute was established.

> However, since the school of law started focusing on social media legal law defenses, there has been a steady increase in the number of protests there, usually in relation to the school issuing statements in support of the current Internet "darling company" and their recent IPO.

Technology

▶ The Fugate Institute's main data center is housed in the 100 Washington Avenue building.

▷ It occupies one-half of the 3rd floor.

▷ It contains more than 200 servers running 85 separate applications to serve various departments, processes, and research labs.

▷ The Technology Division has outsourced their network services to eNetwerk.

> Although support is outsourced, the network equipment still resides in this data center.

> There is a project underway to move all networking equipment to an e-Netwerk facility in Detroit; this is due to be completed next month.

▶ The company runs an intranet and an extranet; they own the Fugate.edu domain.

▷ In order to protect their brand, they also own fugateinstitute.edu, fugateinst.edu, fugateschool.edu, and fug8.edu. They also purchased the .com, .net and .biz versions of these names.

▶ The Todd School's data center currently houses its network facilities and its legal database (FindLegal).

▷ As part of the school's overall strategy to outsource network functions, Todd's network is scheduled to move to Detroit as well, over the same weekend. Some network migration has already begun.

▷ The FindLegal application is also scheduled to migrate to the school's new data center in Milwaukee.

Disaster recovery strategy

▶ Approximately two months after the scheduled network move (see above), the entire data center is also scheduled to move into a brand new facility in Milwaukee,

FUGATE INSTITUTE continued on next page

FUGATE INSTITUTE continued from previous page

Wisconsin.

▷ With the network moving and the data center moving, no one seems to have noticed that the disaster recovery contract with WeRent4U is due to expire in three weeks.

▶ The WeRent4U contract provides hotsite services.

▷ The nearest hotsite location is in Toledo, Ohio.

▷ The contract does not provide for a designated work area recovery space.

> There is a provision for mobile work area trailers to be brought in.

> The closest area large enough to accommodate the trailers is approximately one-half mile away (and across the river) from the Washington Avenue building complex.

▶ The DR strategy varies by system or application tier.

▷ Tier One application data is replicated in near-real-time to WeRent4U, with once daily tape back-ups sent to MoonGuard.

> Only three applications are designated as Tier One (student info, ResearchTrak, and FindLegal).

▷ All other applications have tape back-ups taken either daily or weekly and sent to MoonGuard.

> Although MoonGuard has facilities across the state, for ease of access, Fugate has chosen to store its tapes at the MoonGuard facility, located two blocks south of the data center on Washington Avenue.

▷ Recovery from tape has been tested for isolated applications, never more than one application at a time.

Communications

▶ Thanks to the recent financial difficulties and unfortunate attention to a luxury home development project that the Williams family had invested heavily in (the family is estimated to have lost over $1 billion in the project), the MarComm Division (Marketing and Communications) has recently contracted with two new communications and marketing specialists to supplement their existing overworked specialist.

▷ The school has been busy trying to find additional financial sources for research projects, as the current endowment lost over 40% of its value in the past year.

▷ The Division believes the need for these two additional specialists will be temporary.

FUGATE INSTITUTE continued on next page

FUGATE INSTITUTE continued from previous page

Crisis communications plan

▶ The Fugate Institute has a very informal crisis communications plan in place.
 ▷ There are very rough guidelines on what not to say and how not to say it.
 ▷ Overall, the Communications Department believes they can react quickly to any event that arises.

MOCK COMPANIES

American One Financial Services, Inc.

Introduction and company history

American One Financial Services, Inc., (NASDAQ: AM1) is a financial services company in 12 states, offering everything from individual direct-deposit accounts and safe deposit boxes at its branches, to institutional investment services for medium-sized and large corporate clients.

It was chartered in 1992 in Ohio, Kentucky, and West Virginia, and expanded into Illinois in 1995. Its growth into nine other states and into other financial service areas (insurance, auto leasing, corporate investment, etc.) has occurred in the past five years primarily through acquisition of smaller banks and competitors. Some locations have been fully integrated (processes, technology, culture), while most are in varying stages of integration. Integration has not always gone smoothly.

People

- ▶ The company is headquartered in Cleveland, Ohio.
  - ▷ Through their affiliates, they do business in the following states: Ohio, Michigan, Florida, Missouri, Georgia, North Carolina, Illinois, Pennsylvania, Indiana, Tennessee, Kentucky, and West Virginia.
- ▶ The company employs 12,500 direct employees.
  - ▷ Approximately 85% are full-time employees, with the remainder working part-time.
  - ▷ Part-time employees work primarily in the branch offices.
  - ▷ In addition to the direct employees, there is a substantial contractor and temp worker base, approximately 675, with many based at the Cleveland headquarters, in particular, in the Technology Division.
- ▶ In an attempt to keep up with their competition, American One recently opened two additional locations in Europe.
  - ▷ Their Glasgow, Scotland, location is a new, state-of-the-art customer service call center.
  - ▷ The Mumbai, India, location provides support for the company's settlement and treasury processing.
- ▶ Organizational structure:
  - ▷ The Risk Management Division reports up to the Operations Group, and houses the Business Continuity Department and the Financial Risk Department.
  - ▷ The Environmental Health & Safety Department reports to Human Resources, which reports up to the Admin Group.
  - ▷ The disaster recovery function is integrated into the Technology Division,

AMERICAN ONE FINANCIAL continued on next page

AMERICAN ONE FINANCIAL continued from previous page

with all Technology employees cross-trained to perform various recovery activities. It is not an optimal set-up, and the structure has not worked well during emergencies in the past; luckily, those emergencies were relatively minor.

Facilities

▶ The Cleveland headquarters complex:
  ▷ Three buildings: 101 Main Street, 111 Main Street, and 121 Main Street. Most executives occupy the top three floors of 121 Main. The data center is also located in 121 Main.
  ▷ All were built at the same time in 1992, and are separated by one city block.
  ▷ 101 Main is 20 stories tall, 111 Main is 25 stories tall, and 121 Main is 30 stories tall.
  ▷ American One owns the buildings and occupies all floors, with the exception of the ground floor of 101 Main.
    > That floor is rented out to a restaurant, America's Bounty Buffet, and a DrugRite drugstore.
  ▷ There are small cafeterias on the 7th floor of 101 Main and 111 Main; the primary company cafeteria is on the 10th floor of 121 Main.
    > All cafeterias are outsourced to GrazeWell, a local food vendor. The smaller cafeterias have no cooking facilities, and offer only cold sandwiches and salads, while the primary cafeteria offers a pizza station, grill station, and display cooking station, in addition to cold sandwiches and salads.
▶ Cleveland's Main Street runs parallel to a major artery through the city.
  ▷ To the east, the American One buildings overlook both the freeway and a small airport.
  ▷ To the west, they overlook a cruise dock, where pleasure ships leave for short dinner cruises, as well as multiple-day-long Cuyahoga River cruises.
▶ There is a generator for each building; however, they have not been tested in more than two years.
  ▷ The data center in 121 Main has two UPS systems as well as its own generator.
  ▷ The data center generator has not been tested in two years either; all power outages that the company has suffered has been short enough that the UPS have been able to handle them.
▶ There are 1,300 other locations in 12 states.
  ▷ 1,200 are branches, and the remainder are offices for their affiliated companies.

AMERICAN ONE FINANCIAL continued on next page

AMERICAN ONE FINANCIAL continued from previous page

▷ All other locations are rented space, and all other locations share their respective facilities with at least three other companies.

▷ Rented space in these non-headquarters locations ranges from a small 3,000-square-foot, one-story branch in Traverse City, Michigan, to half of a four-story building housing their auto leasing affiliate in Jacksonville, Florida.

Emergency response program

▶ American One has a fairly robust Emergency Response Program in place for their high-rise facilities in Cleveland.

▷ They have enthusiastic floor wardens.

▷ They are required by law to hold one full-building fire drill a year.

> In addition to the annual drill, EHS and the floor wardens hold smaller drills once a month, rotating through the various floors.

▶ American One has not been as successful rolling out a similar robust ERP in its outlying and acquired properties.

▷ Some came with a reasonably strong ERP; those have been maintained.

▷ Most acquisitions had programs ranging from poor to mediocre, and the company has not had much success bringing these up to the same level as the Main Street complex.

Mission-critical activities

▶ As with any company chartered with moving and safeguarding money, the primary business activity of American One is the end-of-day settlement processing.

▷ This includes automated clearinghouse (ACH) transfer processing, and associated reconciliation (settlement recon) reports.

▷ Due to federal banking laws and the charters in the states that they do business, there are heavy penalties for misprocessing.

> This includes incorrect processing, as well as late processing.

> Late processing penalties can run into the millions of dollars for every two hours that a settlement or transfer is delayed.

Business continuity strategy

▶ The company has a contract with WeRent4U to provide a hotsite for American One's technology recovery.

▷ The contract does not provide for a designated work area recovery space.

> There is a provision for mobile work area trailers to be brought in.

AMERICAN ONE FINANCIAL continued on next page

AMERICAN ONE FINANCIAL continued from previous page

> > The closest area large enough to accommodate the trailers is approximately one-half mile away from the Main Street building complex.

▶ The BCP program itself is still in its infancy, and was started by the ACH manager three years ago.

> ▷ A rudimentary BIA was done then, and has not been updated since.
> ▷ Bare-bones Business Continuity Plans were also created at that time but have never been tested.
> ▷ All documentation was done in-house on Word documents and Excel spreadsheets. Formats vary from department to department.
> ▷ Other than experiencing an average of eight bank robberies a year at their branches, there have been no significant disasters requiring the company to declare BCP activation since the company was formed.

Technology

▶ American One's data center is housed in the 121 Main Street building.

> ▷ It occupies three-quarters of the 3rd floor.
> ▷ It contains over 300 servers running 125 separate applications to serve various departments, processes, and locations around the company.
> ▷ The Technology Division has outsourced their network services to eNetwerk.
> > > Although support is outsourced, the network equipment still resides in this data center.
> > > There is a project underway to move all networking equipment to an eNetwerk facility in Detroit; this is due to be completed next month.

▶ The company runs an intranet and an extranet; they own the americanone.com domain.

> ▷ In order to protect their brand, they also own american1.com, amer1can.com, am1.com, and amone.com. They also purchased the .net and .biz versions of these names.

Disaster recovery strategy

▶ Approximately two months after the scheduled network move (see above), the entire data center is also scheduled to move into a new facility in Pittsburgh, Pennsylvania.

> ▷ With the network moving and the data center moving, no one seems to have noticed that the disaster recovery contract with WeRent4U is due to expire in

AMERICAN ONE FINANCIAL continued on next page

AMERICAN ONE FINANCIAL continued from previous page

three weeks.

▶ The WeRent4U contract provides hotsite services.

▷ The nearest hotsite location is in Toledo, Ohio.

▷ The contract does not provide for a designated work area recovery space.

> There is a provision for mobile work area trailers to be brought in.

> The closest area large enough to accommodate the trailers is approximately one-half mile away from the Main Street building complex.

▶ The DR strategy varies by system or application tier.

▷ Tier One application data is replicated in near-real-time to WeRent4U, with once daily tape back-ups sent to MoonGuard.

> Only two applications are designated as Tier One (ACH and settlement recon).

▷ All other applications have tape back-ups taken either daily or weekly and sent to MoonGuard.

> Although MoonGuard has facilities across the state, for ease of access, American One has chosen to store its tapes at the MoonGuard facility two blocks south of the data center on Main Street.

▷ Recovery from tape has been tested for isolated applications, never more than one application at a time.

Communications

▶ Thanks to the recent federal bailout and some unfortunate attention to a luxury cruise that their executives recently took (to celebrate not losing as much money as they had expected in the last fiscal quarter), the MarComm Division (Marketing and Communications) has recently contracted with two new communications and public relations specialists to supplement their two existing, overworked specialists.

▷ The Division believes the need for these two additional specialists will be temporary.

Crisis communications plan

▶ American One has a very informal crisis communications plan in place.

▷ There are very rough guidelines on what not to say and how not to say it.

▷ Overall, the Communications department believes they can react quickly to any event that arise.